MONEY HACKS

How Small Changes Can Save Big Money

Copyright 2014 Ahmed Dawn

All rights reserved. No part of this book may be reproduced, in whole or in part, without the specific written permission of the author, Ahmed Dawn. The author is the sole author of the work, and the sole owner of the copyright.

Disclaimer

The information in this book is for informational purposes only and no information is intended as investment, tax, accounting or legal advice, or as an offer to sell or buy or solicitation of an offer to sell or buy, or as an endorsement, recommendation or sponsorship of any product, company, security, or fund. The author assumes no liability for any inaccurate, delayed or incomplete information, nor for any actions taken in reliance thereon. You bear responsibility for your own financial research and decisions, and should seek the advice of a qualified financial professional before making any financial decision.

MONEY HACKS

How Small Changes Can Save Big Money

AHMED DAWN

Creator of Globally Popular Financial
Blog A Dawn Journal

Also By Ahmed Dawn

Invest Now: A Canadian's Guide to Investing

ABOUT THE AUTHOR

Award-winning author Ahmed Dawn is a City University of New York Economics graduate. The former Financial Advisor now works as a Data Integrity Analyst for a major Canadian wealth management corporation. He created Canada's Personal Finance Website A Dawn Journal (www.adawnjournal.com) to make the world of personal finance easy and accessible for everyone. Invest Now is author's first book. He makes his home in the world-class city of Toronto.

This book is dedicated to all Canadian police officers,
fire fighters, and emergency medical technicians. Your courage
and hard work are an inspiration to all of us.

The art is not in making money, but in keeping it.

– Proverb.

TABLE OF CONTENTS

Preface 1

Introduction 2

PART ONE 5

Chapter One: How to Save Money on Groceries 7

Chapter Two: How to Save Money on Clothing 12

Chapter Three: How to Save Money On Phone 15

Chapter Four: How to Save Money On Internet 18

Chapter Five: How to Save Money on Cable TV 20

Chapter Six: How to Save Money on Transportation 23

Chapter Seven: How to Save Money on Movies 27

Chapter Eight: How to Save Money At Restaurants 29

Chapter Nine: How To Save Money on Lunch 31

Chapter Ten: How to Save Money on Appliances 32

Chapter Eleven: How to Save Money on Extended Warranty 36

PART TWO 39

Chapter Twelve: How to Save Money on Housing 41

Chapter Thirteen: How to Save Money on Mortgage 44

Chapter Fourteen: How to Save Money on Banking Fees 47

Chapter Fifteen: How to Save Money on Credit Cards 50

Chapter Sixteen: How to Save Money on Taxes 54

Chapter Seventeen: How to Save Money on Travel or Vacation 57

Chapter Eighteen: Smart Phone – Your Ticket to Savings 60

Chapter Nineteen: A Dawn Journal 63

Conclusion 74

PREFACE

Everyday, we face tempting opportunities to spend money. Spending is one of the few things in life that is guaranteed to happen from your birth till you die. The art is in spending less, a lot less, just by applying a few simple rules that are unknown to most of us.

These rules are not hard to apply, and you should not have to go through a 400-page book to start saving your money. In Money Hacks, I will walk you through with my no-nonsense, pragmatic approach to saving in simple and understandable terms, so you can start saving right away from page one, day one.

Our main problem is lack of information. There are some tips and tricks the manufacturers, service providers, and your supermarkets don't want you to know. You will find lots of those in Money hacks. And I will also take you beyond just applying some simple tips and tricks. Equipped with your newly-obtained knowledge, you will be more confident when you walk into your grocery store the next time.

You are the domain of your financial future. Start saving extra money today. The extra money you save, start investing (Please refer to Invest Now to enhance your knowledge on investing!) them toward a better future. This is your future and no one else will do it for you. What you save and invest today will have enormous impact in the future. Don't wait – do it now – Save Now. This is the time.

INTRODUCTION

Why This Book?

If you walk into a grocery supermarket or a big retailer like Costco, you will find hundreds of people are pouring endless stuff in their shopping carts. Only a handful of this stuff is actually necessity items. Most of the other stuff they are paying for and bringing home aimlessly without even knowing that they were tricked into buying something they do not need. They were promised that they were going to save money by buying bulk. Very few consumers are aware of how stores trick us to pay more in the name of saving money. This is where Money Hacks comes in to provide you that knowledge you need to shop smart and save money as long as you live. Walk into your store with confidence the next time you go shopping. The difference between someone who does not have that knowledge and you will be dramatic.

Stop Right Now and Don't Buy Money Hacks

This book will not do any good if you just read this book and put it on your shelf once you are done with it, without applying anything mentioned in it. If your intention is not to use the procedures described here and just to buy this book for the sake of buying, I ask you to stop right now, do not buy this book, and save some money.

Money Hacks Is Not A Get Rich Scam or A Promise to Make You A Millionaire

Yes, Money Hacks will show you how to save money. However, if you are expecting to be an instant millionaire, this is not the right book for you. I ask you to move on and try something else.

Frequently Asked Questions

If you have read my first book Invest Now, you already know that I like to do things differently. Introductions do not usually feature a FAQ section, but I started adding FAQ section in Invest Now and the same will continue for Money Hacks. So here I will answer some basic questions you may have about me and Money Hacks through these frequently asked questions.

Who are you?

I am the author of award-winning book Invest Now. Also, I am the author of several other websites. Among them, popular personal finance website www.adawnjournal.com attracts thousands of visitors across the globe daily.

Why is this book so thin?

Have you heard of information overload? In this digital age, we are always bombarded with information and our capacity allows us to grasp and use only so much. If you read a 400-page book with money-saving tips, what you will likely to do at the end? You will just put it on your shelf to collect dust. I have eliminated chitchat, small talk, and stories of John and Jane, organising the book with only the stuff you need to know.

How much money will I will save?

This is a hard question to answer, honestly. How much money you will save mainly depends on your lifestyle and spending habits. Each chapter will represent different dollar amounts savings for different individuals. However, I will tell you this with confidence that only applying two chapters (how to save money on Internet and how to save money on cable) can save you at least $100 per month.

OK, I like your writing style explaining simply how to save. How can I get more of your articles or follow up with you beyond this book?

I am the author of popular financial website A Dawn Journal at www.adawnjournal.com which attracts thousands of readers daily across the globe. I suggest you visit A Dawn Journal on a regular basis for more articles on money saving and investing. I also write on other websites on a variety of topics. You will find links to these sites on the right panel of A Dawn Journal.

PART ONE

CHAPTER ONE

How to Save Money on Groceries

Let's Begin

I have decided to start Money Hacks with money-saving tips on groceries. You may not realise it, but grocery bills take out a big chunk of our budget, every day, month after month – although it may not seem that way.

I am presenting a few tips for you to follow and save money. You may not be able to use all of these tips. Just use those that make sense for you.

Avoid Worst Times to Go Grocery Shopping

Avoid going to grocery stores during these times: Friday evening to Sunday, weekdays two hours before and after 5, and the day before long weekend. Why? Because you will face the most crowds, it will be hard to find products on sale, and you will be in a rush – leading you to miss items that offer the best value.

Pay Attention to Unit Pricing

If you have not noticed those tiny per unit prices yet, it is time to check those closely. Just because an item is on sale, it does not mean it's cheap. For example, if you check the unit price of a big container of orange juice, most likely it will be cheaper than a medium container of orange juice on sale.

Leave the Kids At Home

Kids will always want to buy items that aren't on your list and it's hard to always tell them NO when they pick up something. Leave the kids at home and it will be a lot easier to concentrate on buying only what you need.

Make A List and Don't Buy If It's Not On List

If you go shopping without a list, you will end up buying what you don't need. A list helps you finish your task your task quickly, thus saving money.

Concentrate on Items on Sale, But With Caution

Always try to buy more items that are on sale. However, do not blindly buy items because they are on sale. Sometimes items on sale are not really bargains, as stores jack up their prices before a sale. It's a good idea to stockpile items when you detect a good sale for future use.

Track Prices of Major Items

This is one of my favourites. I start tracking price for big items such as orange juice, detergent, coffee, and so on. When I find these items on sale, I stockpile them for the coming weeks. You can use the same technique for items such as electronics, household appliances, etc. There are websites that will send you alerts when items are on sale. For example, when I needed a light vacuum cleaner, which is regularly priced at $100, I setup an email alert on the Canadian Tire website. I got an email alert telling me that it was on sale for $40, so I went to the store to pick it up.

Shopping and Emotions

Do not enter a grocery store – or any store – when you are upset, angry, depressed, or feeling too good. Shopaholic people buy products they will never need and never use just to make themselves happy. Do not let your emotion control your action. Nothing can bring you more happiness than sticking to your budget and saving money.

Do Not Spend Money on Junk Beverages

Beverages like soda, fruit punch, colored water, etc. are a waste and bad for your health. Buy pure juices that are not from concentrate when they are on sale. There are many other beverages that are full of nothing else but loaded sugar; avoid these and save your health and money.

Shelves Near The Checkout Counter

Have you ever wondered why they put a variety of unrelated items near the checkout counter? They are there to lure you while you wait in line for the cashier. These items are usually overpriced and small in size, so they are easy to grab while standing or passing the aisle. Avoid these items, as they are there to satisfy impulsive craving.

The Secrets of Eye-Level Shelves

When you are inside a grocery store, your eyes will always stick to those shelves that don't require you to look up or down. Grocery store chains know it very well, and they keep regular prices items on eye-level shelves. However, you are on a mission to save money and you know where to look. Always check those shelves that are located above and below the eye level shelves; you are guaranteed to find bargains there.

Convenience Items Are Inconvenience For Bank Account

Convenience items such as prepacked meals, salads, sandwiches, etc. are always overpriced and bad for both your health and your wallet. You can save a lot of money if you buy ingredients separately and make it yourself.

Bulk Items May Not Make Your Wallet Bulky

Buying items in bulk may seem to be a good idea to save money, but it may not always save you money. Use your common sense to figure out if buying something in bulk makes sense for you. Buying items in bulk for big families makes more sense than small families. For the same reason, buying at Costco for single people or small families makes no sense after paying the annual fees. Also, I don't like to buy the same items in large quantities and use the same thing month after month. For example, would you like to use the same toothpaste month after month?

Don't Be A Slave to Brand Names

Brand name items are always guaranteed to cost you more, but they may not give you better value than generic items. If you cannot leave brand names, try to get them when they are on sale. I like brand name clothes, but instead of buying them at regular price I keep an eye on when they go on sale and buy at that time.

Comparison Shopping

If you live in a city, you have the opportunity to shop at various stores without driving too far, or even within walking distance, instead of going to the only available store in that area. Store A sells meat at cheaper prices – that does not mean that all other items are cheaper at Store A than Store B. Orange juice and milk may be cheaper at Store B, but meat may be more expensive. In my neighbourhood, I have access to 3 different grocery stores and I know what to buy from where to save money.

Tidbits

As you may have noticed, I skipped mentioning cutting coupons to save money. Cutting coupons may work for some, but it has never worked for me. I avoid the hassle of cutting coupons, filling up my wallet with them, and going through them at the checkout to find the right one. If you can deal with coupons to save money, go ahead and do it; but it will not work for everyone.

What works for me are reward or travel point credit cards. Pick a reward or travel point credit card that meets your need and buy everything on that card to accumulate your points faster. If you need help with choosing a credit card, visit www.adawnjournal.com for info to pick one. What I noticed is that my reward card accumulates at an average of $150 or possibly more every year even without my attention. What other way you can make that money legally without doing anything?

CHAPTER TWO

How to Save Money on Clothing

Let's Do Things a Little Differently

Here my tips will be a little different than the traditional tips you will usually get from money coaches. I am sure you heard in the past to avoid brand name clothes and visit thrift shops to save money, but today I will tell you the opposite to save money.

No Name Vs. Brand Name

When it comes to clothing, avoid buying no name, cheap clothes. Instead, buy a few brand name clothes. However, as brand name clothes are expensive, don't pay full price and buy them on sale or from factory outlet stores. Brand name clothes will last longer, fit better, and will be worth paying more in the long run.

I bought a shirt once for $10 thinking it was a bargain. After a few washes, the color ran out and it shrunk so much that it became unwearable. However, I still wear my clothes I bought from well-known stores 10 years ago and I can tell that these will last another five years easily. If I paid $50 or even $100 for one shirt that's going to keep going for so many years, and on the other hand a $10 shirt that does not last one year, do your math and you'll see which one provides more value for your money.

Thrift Store Cloths Aren't Thrift

Some of us may find thrift stores are where you can get bargain deals and save money on clothes. However, the endless time you spend to find something that fits and possibility of defective clothes are not worth the hassle. Also, as these clothes have already been used, they can't outlast new clothes in the long run.

Prolong Life

If you take good care of your clothes, they will last a lot longer than you can possibly imagine. A few simple tricks in the washer and dryer can prolong your clothes' life, such as using medium spin rather than high spin. You can also dry your clothes for a short time rather than the full time and then hang them to dry. This will add years to your clothes' life and keep them looking newer for many years. For delicate clothes, avoid putting them in the washing machine and hand wash and hang dry them instead. Washing and drying in a machine takes years away from clothes and make them look old. However, it may not be realistic to hand wash everything, so wash and dry them using a gentle cycle and heat to get more years from your clothes.

Impulse Buying

Instead of going to the mall and buying clothes indiscriminately, have an annual budget for clothing and make a list of what you will need to buy for every year. This budget should be relevant to your annual income. For example, although my yearly allocation on clothes is $1000, I hardly exceed $500 in a given year.

Never Buy Clothes That Are Not On Sale

All my clothes are brand name clothes with expensive price tags. However, I have never paid what's on the tags. They all last usually somewhere between 5 to 10 years and then I donate these to thrift shops for further use. You can wear expensive clothes without paying expensive prices if you know where to buy. You have to shop around and it should not take long to figure out where you can get bargain clothes in your city. When I lived in New York, I mastered all the stores that sell expensive clothes without expensive price tags. After moving to Toronto, it took me about a year to figure out where to go to shop. You don't have to wait for Black Friday or Boxing Day to get sales. If you search enough, you will find out that there are sales happening every month and every day. There is no point paying full price when you can pay 30 to 60 percent less for the same. You just have to look around.

CHAPTER THREE

How to Save Money On Phone

In this chapter, I will cover both home and cell (mobile) phone. I have seen people paying $80 to $100 for their cell phone and $50 to $60 for their home phone. The first thing I will say is: Stop this madness! After reading this chapter, if you can make your combined phone bill within $50, I would give you an excellent rating. If it's $100, I would say, "It's not bad, but there is room for improvement."

Eliminate Your Home Phone

These days, it makes sense to cut off the cord to your home phone and save $30 to $60 monthly. Unless your circumstances require you to absolutely have a home phone, such as you have elderly parents living at home, home phones are becoming obsolete. If you would still like to have that home phone feeling using a cell phone but without a home phone service, use devices such as cellular Bluetooth gateway. These devices let you make and receive calls from your home phone using your cell phone service. However, if you still can't leave traditional home phone services, try the following to save money.

Call the Retentions Department

Most of the big phone companies have a specialized department to handle rogue and disobedient customers who are about to leave for a better deal. This department is called the Retentions Department. Talk to your phone company's Retentions Department and tell them that you are considering cutting off your home phone because you can't afford it anymore or switching to the other phone company because they are offering a better deal and you are calling to find out if you can get a better deal because you would like to stay with your current phone company. Ninety percent of the time you will end up with a better rate than what you have been paying. When I had to have a home phone because of my parents, I called them every year to put me on a deal. The reason you need to call every year is because phone companies will not give you a discounted deal for more than a year, so you need to call every year and make them keep you as their customer.

Use Your Computer/Tablet/Smartphone As A Phone Without A Service Provider

The Internet has revolutionized communications and it is time to take advantage of it. There are various apps you can use on your computer, tablet, or smartphone that can give you a real phone number with all the features like a cell phone using WiFi, but without the service charges like regular phones. Search for "free calls" on Google Play under Apps and you will see many of these free phone apps. Groove and Fongo are two such examples. It is possible to make and receive calls or texts on your cell phone, tablet, or computer now without paying service providers as long as you have access to WiFi. This opens up the opportunity to have a free Internet phone service for those who can't afford to pay for phone service.

Use Discount Phone Service Providers

In any country, there are discount phone service providers in addition to regular pricey phone service providers that offer the same services at a fraction of the cost. There are not many differences in terms of what you are getting from regular providers, and you can even get a lot more features with these small companies at a price that big companies will not be able to match. For example, in Canada you can get everything unlimited, including data and global text, from Wind Mobile for around $50 per month. You can get a similar plan from big players like Rogers for more than $100 a month, but they will never give you unlimited data. You can save a lot if you have access to small, discounted providers in your area.

Combine Your Plans

Check with your provider to see if they provide discounts for bundling or combining your plans. What this means is that instead of taking services such as Internet, cell phone, home phone, cable, etc. from different providers, you will be taking it from the same provider and receive discounts. If your provider offers no such discounts, look for another provider.

Keep An Eye Open

Even if you are satisfied with your current provider, don't stop keeping an eye on promotions from other providers. What I noticed is that before Christmas or other big religious days there are lots of promotions going on from providers to sign up customers. This is your ideal time to switch to a better deal and save money. Also, look out for when new providers enter the market. For the first few months, new entrants offer ridiculous deals to hook up customers.

CHAPTER FOUR

How to Save Money On Internet

Use Your Cell Phone's Internet

The best way to save money on Internet is not to have a separate Internet service, save at least $50 monthly, and still have high-speed Internet. Is this really possible? Yes, it is. I discontinued my regular Internet service in January 2011 and save at least $50 a month. To have Internet for free, you need to have an unlimited data plan on your cell phone and use your cell phone's Internet for your computers and laptops.

If you have an Android phone with an unlimited data plan, you will have to check on Portable WiFi hotspot (this can be found under settings) and your smartphone will work as a router to supply your other devices Internet wirelessly. However, there are some disadvantages to use Internet for free this way. One is that your phone has to stay at home to provide Internet to other devices and you have to have unlimited Internet with good speed. If this is not an option for you, move on to the next tip.

How To Save Money on Internet Otherwise

The same as small cell phone providers, look for small Internet providers in your area. They probably will not have 24-hour customer service like big providers, but the money you will be saving is astounding. In some instances, small providers actually will give you the same Internet as the big companies, but at a fraction of the cost.

How is this done? Many small Internet companies cannot afford to have their own Internet services, so they lease from the big guys and resell them at discounted costs. Examples of this type of third-party Internet providers in Canada would be Start Communications or TekSavvy.

Lower One Level of Service

There are various levels of services you can buy from your Internet provider. Different providers have different names for these, but generally it goes like light, medium, express, ultra express, etc. If you subscribe to something other than the lowest one, you can easily switch to one level lower service and will be able to save money. Most likely you will not even notice the slightly lower speed, but the savings will add up month after month.

CHAPTER FIVE

How to Save Money on Cable TV

Not to Have Cable At All

The best way to save money on cable is not to have cable service at all. However, it does not mean you have to give up watching TV. By law, broadcasters have to broadcast digital signals over the air now and that means you can watch super quality over-the-air high definition TV without spending a cent. All you need is a TV and an antenna. Most of the popular channels are available over-the-air such as CBC, CBS, NBC, CTV, Fox, OMNI, WNED, and so on. The picture and sound quality in fact will be better than cable because unlike cable TV, the signal is not compressed when it's over-the-air. However, you will have to give up some channels that are only available on cable such as The Weather Channel, TSN, Showtime, etc.

If you live in an apartment or a condo, all you have to do is to buy an indoor over-the-air antenna to receive a digital high-definition signal for free. Your estimated one-time cost to buy an antenna will be about $40 to $100. Antennas have come a long way these days. There are indoor antennas you can buy which look like a book or an iPad and lie flat on any surface near the window to give you amazing reception.

If you live in a house, your one-time cost might be little bit higher if you need to install an outdoor antenna. If you can install it by yourself, you are looking at spending around $300 to $500. Stores like Home Depot and Canada Computers have everything you need to buy and install your outdoor antenna.

If you don't want to go through the hassle of buying and installing an outdoor antenna by yourself, you can ask a professional installer to do it for you. They will be able to do everything for you for around $500 to $1000. To find a professional antenna service near you, search online for "install over the air antenna."

One last thing: Don't be intimidated by the one-time cost to setup an antenna. Although there are some initial costs, you will recover it within a few months and it will be free after that for every month, year after year.

Call Your Cable Company

If you must have a cable service, here are some tips to save you money. Call your cable company and tell them that you can't afford to pay this much for cable and you would like to terminate your plan. But before that, you are calling to find out if they can put you on a promotion so you can keep your cable. Does this really work? Yes, it woks. When I had cable service, I always enjoyed paying 35-40% less just by calling them and saying the above. If by any chance you ended up getting a rogue customer service rep that does not want to cooperate, don't give up and ask for a supervisor or manager. If still you are out of luck with a manager (although I doubt you will), at the last moment say you will think it over for a few more days and end your conversation. Call back and try the same again after 2/3 weeks.

Switch To A Different provider

Call each provider in your area and switch to whichever one offers you the best rates.

Degrade Your Service

Do you really have time to watch 50 regular channels and 5 premier channels? Check your cable bill and see what's included and what you are using. Call your cable company and ask them to switch you to a lower package that still suits your needs and saves you money.

Try Alternate Options

Sites like Hulu, Crackle, and Netflix offer movies, TV shows, and much more for free or for a minimal monthly fee. You can watch these on smart TV or on a regular TV with a cheap device called Chromecast. Also, smart TV has apps that offer premier TV channels at a lower cost than having cable service. There are more and more free services becoming available on a wider scale. All you need to enjoy TV without cable service is to have a smart TV (or a regular TV with a streaming device) and unlimited Internet. There are lots of opportunities to save money when you know how to do it. It's no wonder cable companies are losing customers and desperate to launch their own streaming services.

CHAPTER SIX

How to Save Money on Transportation

In this chapter, I will cover related topics such as saving money on a car, public transportation, saving money on gas, etc. Let's begin with public transportation.

Public Transportation

This is your best option to save money, if you have to commute. Years ago, I gave my Toyota Celica to charity and have been using public transportation ever since. It could save you thousands of dollars every year, year after year. If you have access to public transportation, consider using it and save money and cut back on your carbon emission.

If you use public transportation several times daily and on the weekends, you might be better off buying a monthly pass than paying each time. Don't forget to check if your city offers a tax credit for using a monthly transit pass. This will even lower your costs of using public transit further.

Save Money on a Car

Buy Used Cars: Buying a one to five year-old car gives you an almost-new car for a fraction of the cost. A new car depreciates about 35 percent when you drive it off the lot.

Brand Matters: Some brands depreciate more than other brands. You don't want to buy a car that is high on depreciation. Search online to check which brands depreciate faster using these keywords: "car resale value" or "car depreciation."

Buy Hybrid or Smaller Cars: Hybrid cars are no longer expensive like they used to be. Many countries also offer a special tax credit for buying hybrid cars. Also, smaller cars are popular these days. These kinds of cars will save you a lot of money on gas for the life of the car. Compare fuel efficiency among different makes and models before buying a car.

Save Money on Gas

Shop Around: Gas prices can vary based on the area and the day of the week. Gas stations in an upscale neighbourhood are likely to have higher gas prices. Also, price fluctuates based on the day of the week. Fill up your car from Monday through Thursday and avoid filling up from Friday through Sunday. Use websites or smartphone apps like GasBuddy to compare prices before heading to the gas station. As of this writing, the lowest and highest gas prices listed in my area of Toronto, Canada are 124.9 and 130.0 cents per litre. Yes, the small differences can lead to big savings if you fill up your tank.

Use Regular Gas: There is no point in using premium gas, unless your vehicle manufacturer specifically you to not use regular gas. Research shows that using premium gas for regular cars will not provide you any benefits, except it is draining more money down the hose.

Use A Gas Rebate Credit Card: This type of credit card gives cash back for buying gas or regular merchandise. The savings can be huge if you buy everything you would buy anyway on this credit card. To find a suitable card for you, search online for "gas rebate credit card" and pick the one that best meets your needs.

Empty Your Car Trunk: An empty car trunk translates into less gas. Do not keep anything in your trunk that you don't need.

Mind the Speed Limit. Driving above 60 mph/100 kmh will cost you the most, as it's not gas efficient. Staying within the speed limit saves money, saves gas, and saves getting costly speed tickets as well.

Avoid Idling: Idling more than 2-3 minutes costs you money. In some areas, it is unlawful to idle a car. If you need to stay in car for a while, shut off the engine and save money.

Never Empty Your Tank: Fill up the tank before it's fully empty. Cars run better when the tank is half or more than half full. An almost-empty tank costs more money.

Avoid Harsh Driving: Driving at a smooth and balanced pace saves you gas and gives your car a longer life. Be easy on your break and gas pedal and save money.

Maintain Your Car Properly

To keep your car in good condition and save on gas, do these regularly:

- Keep your tires properly inflated.
- Check and replace air and fuel filters regularly.
- Tune up your car when necessary.
- Avoid additives.
- Turn off air conditioner
- Do routine oil change (for motor and transmission).
- Do routine break fluid change.

Save Money on Insurance

Before You Buy: Instead of deciding on one model, pick a few models, and then check how each of these will cost you to insure. Pick the one with the lowest insurance cost.

Shop Around: Use insurance comparison websites to get the best rates. Search online by entering the keywords "car insurance quotes." Also, you may want to try an insurance advisor to get deals that will be unavailable to you. Unlike mortgage brokers, insurance brokers are not free. However, you will recover your fees paid to them if they can bring you a good deal.

Evaluate Your Situation: Evaluate if you need to have collision and comprehensive covering or can go with only liability coverage. Do you need to increase your deductible or do you need to keep it minimal? Deciding on these factors can save you significantly.

Group Insurance: Check if your work offers discounted insurance plans for employees.

Bundle Up: If you have more than one insurance product to carry, as most of us do, check with your insurance company to see if there are discounts for bundling up. If there are none, switch to someone who offers bundling up or package deals.

CHAPTER SEVEN

How to Save Money on Movies

In this chapter, instead of discussing alternative movie tips such as subscribing to Netflix or checking out a movie at movie kiosk, I will stick to real movie theatre tips.

Find Your Local Movie Deal

Depending on where you live and what movie theatres are available, most likely they have a special deal day or time to offer movies at discounted rates. In my area, a movie is only $4 every Tuesday – all day long. Some other places, the deal could be any day as long as you are watching before 4.00 P.M. Check what's available in your area and utilize those time frames to save money.

Join A Movie Reward Program

In Canada, we have a reward program that offers points for watching movies. You get to see your 11th movie for free once you accumulate points from watching ten movies. Furthermore, sometimes you can get bonus points and the free movie comes even faster. Find a movie reward program in your country and save money on movies. There are some credit cards that also offer free movies by giving you points when you shop with those movie reward cards. Along with a movie reward program and a movie reward card, you can save even more on movies.

Avoid The Concession Booth

Avoid concession booths or stands at theatres at any cost. Just like airport food stalls, movie concession stands are a total rip off. Why would you want to pay $10 for a coke and popcorn? Have your snacks or coffee before coming to theatre and save money.

CHAPTER EIGHT

How to Save Money At Restaurants

Eating out is expensive, but it is unrealistic to stop eating out completely to save money. However, following at least one or more tips mentioned in this chapter will save you some money.

Avoid Beverages

Beverages are one of the highest mark-up items at restaurants, especially alcoholic beverages. If you can cut down on beverages at restaurants, you will be able to cut down on your bills too. Besides, water is a lot better for you than sugary and alcoholic drinks.

Eat Out With Friends & Family

This is simple economics of scale. If you eat alone, you will be paying more per person. The reason you will be paying less person with friends and family because you can share dishes, and there is no need to order one dish for each person. For example, if five people are eating out, ordering three dishes will be more than enough for five people.

Look For Deal Day

Most restaurants have a day when they offer reductions on selected items. Some restaurants might offer deals everyday on selected items. Knowing when and which restaurants offer these deals will save you money.

Lunch Is Always Cheaper

Lunch will always cost less than dinner. Lunch menus will have less items available than dinner menus, but the savings will be significantly higher.

And Remember These

Appetizers and desserts are unnecessary and wasteful. Leftovers should not be left behind. Combo meals cost less than individually picked items. And always plan ahead and stay within your budget.

CHAPTER NINE

How To Save Money on Lunch

The added cost of buying lunch everyday can be staggering once you look at the full picture in terms of gross money you are spending. Let's visualize it in real dollar amounts:

Weekly lunch cost at $10 daily = $10 X 5 = $50

Monthly cost = $50 X 4 = $200

Yearly cost = $200 X 12 = $2400

Now the trick is $2400 spent is not really $2400. You need to look at it in gross dollar amount, meaning how much of your salary before taxes you would have required to spend $2400 net. If you are in a 32% tax bracket (which is low, most people are in higher tax brackets), for example, you keep 68% of each additional dollar you earn. What it means is that saving $2400 annually actually saves you $3500 in pre-tax savings. Let's put it another way – if you can skip buying lunch, it's like giving yourself a $3500 annual raise.

If you can't pack lunch everyday, pack at least two to three times a week.

CHAPTER TEN

How to Save Money on Appliances

Appliances are expensive and can cost you a fortune if you need to buy a few of them at the same time. Here are some tips to help you with shopping for your appliances next time.

Ask For Discounts

I know it sounds easy, but most of us don't know and never ask for additional discounts on appliances from the sales associates you are dealing with. Actually, I regret not knowing it sooner as well. About ten years ago, I paid what's on the tag just like other customers at the stores.

Sales associates are authorized to give special discounts at big stores, but you have to ask for it. I usually deal with the same guy to buy large items like appliances or electronics. I get 20 to 30 percent off on anything I buy. But it does not stop there; he also cuts me deals on delivery and extended warranties.

The reason he does not want to lose me because these associates work on commissions, not salaries. So the more he can sell, the more he can make, even giving me off-book discounts. Now, what's happening is that my relatives and friends buy large items from him as well, once I introduced them to him. Everyone wins.

Wait For A Sale

If you need to replace an old appliance that's about to die at any moment, do not wait until the last moment for it to die. If you wait, whenever it breaks down you may not have options to shop around and wait for a deal and will end up paying a higher price. Make an estimate when you want to replace your old appliance and start searching for deals a few months ahead.

To buy an item on sale, you don't need to wait for Christmas or major holidays to get deals. All retailers run promotions throughout the year at different times. Keep an eye on several stores sales and buy once you find one.

Moreover, do not stop keeping an eye on sales even after you finish buying. Most stores have a 30-day price guarantee period. If the same item gets lower after your purchase within 30 days, you will get back the difference. I got about $35 refund on my TV in 2014 and $100 refund on my laptop in 2013 after I had purchased them. The only reason I got back my money because I was still checking prices after I had bought them for 30 days.

Visit Floor Models or Clearing Sections

Every store, even Ikea, has a section where they showcase discontinued, returned, or last year models at lower prices. Some of these items are slightly visually imperfect due to dents or scratches, but in perfectly working condition. Some of these items have nothing wrong with them, except they were on display and collecting dust, or their packages got ripped or torn during transportation.

Stores offer full warranty on this type of item, just like regular items. If you don't mind the minor issues with floor models or clearing models, these offer great value and great savings.

No-Payment-No-Interest

Ninety nine percent of the time you will find you will find no-payment-no-interest deals on appliances or electronics. If you know how to handle this offer, you can save and make money with this deal.

No-payment-no-interest deals can last from 6 months to 2 years, depending on the store. They will charge you a $50 or $60 administration fee to have this offer. If you have a large item to purchase, this fee should not be a problem, as your savings will offset it. For example, if you have purchased a $2000 item with $60 fees, it's like paying 3 percent interest a year. However, if you save this $2000 and buy an ETF that generates more than 3 percent annually, you will be in a gain position. Visit www.adawnjournal.com ETF section for some ETF and mutual fund ideas. If you don't want to invest, you can pay off high interest debts such as like a credit card or car loan that charges 20 percent interest and save on interest charges.

However, you need to be careful with no-interest-no-payment deals. If you are not utilizing the savings to earn more than what you are paying in fees, it's better to pay it in full. Something important to remember is that you must pay off your full balance before the expiration date. If you are late by even one day or short by one dollar, your no-interest-no-payment deal will be invalid and most retailers will charge you about 30 percent interest since day 1.

I love no-payment-no-interest deals and use it if the amount is bigger. As of this writing, I have approximately a $7000 balance on some appliances I bought. My interest cost comes about 1 percent after factoring in my admin fees. I invested this money in a low risk ETF and on a very conservative estimate I am expecting to make 5 percent on this amount before I need to pay it back.

CHAPTER ELEVEN

How to Save Money on Extended Warranty

I don't like to spend more money on extended warranty for some items I buy. However, for some big-ticket items, you do need an extended warranty. For example, items like washing machines, refrigerators, ovens, big screen TVs, etc.

I understand all items come with a manufacturer's warranty for at lease one year. However, you don't want to go through the hassle and pain of returning some big items. That's unrealistic. In this chapter, let's briefly go over some of the things you need to know to save money on an extended warranty.

Yes or No

The most important part is deciding to get an extended warranty or not. For large and expensive items like I mentioned above, you will be better off getting extended warranty. When I bought my large screen Panasonic HD TV in 2006, it broke down twice within its first year. Because I had paid $300 for an extended warranty for five years, I did not have to worry about taking the TV back to the store or sending it back to Panasonic. I only had to make a phone call and technicians came over to fix it on the spot. According to the estimates I got from those guys, each time it would have cost me more than $500 to fix it had I not had the warranty.

If you are buying comparatively smaller or cheaper items such as laptops, tablets, smartphones, and so on, it won't make sense to get an extended warranty. For example, spending $100 on a warranty for a

$600 laptop or $20 on a $150 tablet is unnecessary. These kinds of items are light and easy to take it back to the store or manufacturer for repairing.

Use The Right Credit Card

There are credit cards that double the manufacturer's warranty for free. For example, if you get a one-year warranty that comes with it, your credit card will add another additional year. If anything happens in the second year, the credit card will reimburse you for all the expenses you have incurred repairing or fixing the item.

This is a very good feature to get from credit cards, but the problem is most of us never use it either because we never think of it or lose our receipts. Get accustomed to what you are getting from your credit cards and utilize those fully to save money. And yes, always save receipts for at least two years in a safe place.

Get An Extended Warranty For Free

There are retailers these days who will refund the extended warranty cost in full either in cash or as store credit if you did not use it. When you are spending lots of money on warranties, shop around or ask which retailers offer this type of deal. These can add up very fast if you don't exercise any warranties.

For example, I had to buy an oven, washing machine, and dryer and the cost of five-year warranties were close to $1000. However, I never needed to use those warranties. As a result, when I buy any item in the future, I already have close to $1000 towards my next purchase. Check in your country which dealers offer this type of warranty. You can save a lot of money in the end.

PART TWO

CHAPTER TWELVE

How to Save Money on Housing

Housing is the largest component of your living expenses. Being the largest also offers the highest potential for savings. However, I might disappoint you by saying there is no easy answer or tip on how to save money on housing. Contrary to popular belief, buying a house may not be the best option to save money for some of you and the reverse can be true as well, as everyone's situation is unique. However, having said that, I will still give you some tips to save money. It is up to you to decide which – buying or renting – will save you money based on your own situations.

When To Rent

If you have not come up with enough savings for a down payment, if your job requires frequent moving from place to place, or if you don't want to stick to one house or condo for a while, renting may be the perfect option for you. Renting will give you freedom, flexibility, and worry-free living, which will hard to achieve in living your own house or condo.

When To Rent

If you saved up enough for a handsome down payment, you don't see yourself moving in the short term, and your earnings should be enough to pay your mortgage in such a way that you can see yourself sometime in the future when you would be able to make a final payment and clear your mortgage to own the house outright, then you may be ready to buy a house. Don't forget that owning a home can cost about 10 to 20 percent more monthly than renting. Also, it is generally accepted that you should buy a home that costs no more than five times what you earn in a year.

Buying A Home May Not Be As Lucrative As It Sounds

You always thought buying a home is the best investment option and beats everything in the long run, right? Think again. A study done by City University of New York professor Jack Clark Francis and Yale's Robert G. Ibbotson shows that over the long run (1978 – 2004) stocks generated 13.4 percent annualized return. However, real estate generated only 8.6 percent. Another research by Yale professor Robert Shiller points out even gloomier real estate return at 3 percent – slightly above the inflation rate.

You may not be missing out that much by not buying a house than if you are properly invested. If you don't know how to invest, read my book Invest Now (available at all online retailers), check out my global financial site A Dawn Journal, or consult a fee-based financial professional.

Use Online Tools & Buy-or-Rent Calculator

There are many online tools and calculators available for free to figure out whether you should buy or rent your home. On A Dawn Journal there is a list of 30 free tools and calculators as well. Here is the url: http://adawnjournal.com/personal-finance-and-investing/30-free-canadian-financial-tools-and-calculators

Using these tools, you will easily able be to find out the long-term costs of buying or renting, if you can afford to buy, how much your mortgage will be, and much more. Before you jump into buying your home, take time to do thorough research.

Consult A Professional

It is a good idea to consult a professional such as a mortgage broker or real estate broker to look at our unique situations and assess if you can afford to carry a mortgage and if you will be better off buying or not.

CHAPTER THIRTEEN

How to Save Money on Mortgage

Having a mortgage can be something that keeps going, going, and going without any end in sight. Your objective should be to shorten the lifespan of your mortgage Here are some easy things you can do to make your mortgage efficient and shorter.

Start With A Bigger Down Payment

If you start with a bigger down payment than the minimum required down payment, you will end up saving lots of money paid in interest. Also, your mortgage life will be a lot shorter.

Increase The Frequency

Increase your mortgage frequency from monthly to accelerated bi-weekly. This simple frequency change can save you years off from your mortgage and thousands of dollars. For example, if you have $100,000 mortgage at 5 percent interest for 25 years, changing frequency from monthly to accelerated bi-weekly will save you $12,437.31 in interest costs and about 4 years.

Make Additional Payments

Whenever possible, make extra payments towards your mortgage. Received a $4000 tax refund? If you don't have other high interest loans, put it into your mortgage. Got a bonus this year? Instead of spending it on a big screen TV, add it to your mortgage.

Do Not Lower Payments

When you renew your mortgage, you will likely have lower payments because you already paid some balance. However, keeping the payment as before will shorten your mortgage life faster.

Raise Payments

If you get a raise or your business makes more money, bump up your mortgage payment in line with your increased income.

Use A Mortgage Broker

A lot of us avoid mortgage brokers, thinking we need to pay them fees or they will trick us and put in a bad deal to make money. However, these assumptions are not true. A good mortgage broker will try heart-and-soul to bring you the best possible deals that you would not have found by yourself. Mortgage brokers make money whenever you get a mortgage and they make more money from repeat clients. Most of these guys get more clients through word of mouth. If they give you a sloppy deal, it's not good for their business in the long term.

My mortgage broker secured a mortgage for me from a financial institution that I had never heard of before and I would not have gotten that by myself. As a result, I was so satisfied that I referred my friends and family to him and he has become our permanent mortgage specialist.

Save on CMHC Fees

In Canada, if your down payment is more than 20 percent, you will not have to pay CMHC (Canada Mortgage and Housing Corporation) mortgage insurance – a significant saving. Visit the CMHC website for more.

Use Online Mortgage Tools

There are lots of free mortgage tools and calculators available online. Use these and try different variable inputs to see how can you save more money. Also, visit A Dawn Journal Real Estate & Mortgage Section to find out more. Here is the url: http://adawnjournal.com/category/economy-mortgage-101

Fixed or Variable

Be careful about picking the fixed or mortgage term. In general, variable term mortgage has lower interest rate than fixed term. However, it does not mean variable term will always be the right one. There are many factors, such as where the interest rates are heading tied to picking up a mortgage rate. Talk to a mortgage professional and based on your situation and current market circumstances, picking the right one will save you a lot of money.

Live In A Smaller Space

One of the many benefits of living in a smaller space is your mortgage will be smaller as well and it saves you money for as long as you live.

CHAPTER FOURTEEN

How to Save Money on Banking Fees

Is it necessary to have a chapter on banking fees in a condensed book like Money Hacks? I think it is, because many of us still pay banking fees without knowing that you can eliminate banking fees completely from your life.

Use A Free Checking Account

Virtual banks are banks without brick-and-mortar locations and offer full phase banking with the fees. These days, these virtual banks offer everything just like physical banks, except that you can't walk into a branch or deal face-to-face with a live person. You have to do everything online or on the phone. I have been using virtual banking for 10+ years and I never had to see a live person.

If you can do it, virtual banks can save you about $100 to $1200 annually, year after year. My virtual bank even gives me free cheques and free points to buy free groceries – just for banking with them for free. So what happens is that I easily accumulate $200 to $300 every 2/3 years for free and use it to buy groceries or clothes. Is this real? Yes, it is. If you are in Canada, you already are familiar with this bank called President Choice Financial. And you will find many other banks like this in other parts of the world.

What If You Want A Physical Bank?

Regardless of how sweet the deal sounds, many of you won't do banking without going to a branch, or some places simply don't have virtual banking services. This is also fine, as long as you are not paying anything. Use the below techniques to save money.

Free Banking By Maintaining A Minimum Balance

All brick-and-mortar banks offer free banking if you keep a minimum balance. Check all banks in your area to find out which one has the lowest minimum requirement with the features that will meet your banking needs.

Combine Accounts

Banks are willing to offer you a deal if you have several products with the same bank such as chequing account, savings account, mortgage, insurance, investment account, etc. Check with your bank or other banks to find out if you can get a deal to cut on banking fees.

Just Ask

You may find it hard to believe, but your friendly banker or financial advisor at your branch has the ability to offer you no-fee banking or reduced-fee banking. If you have a good relationship with your branch, they will not hesitate to give you a deal to make you happy. All you need is to ask.

Common Sense Banking

If you are indeed unable to avoid banking fees, use common sense to do your banking. For example, if you are limited to a certain numbers of transactions at bank teller or at ATM machines, stay within your monthly limit. Don't use the ATM to withdraw $20 cash 5 times when you can do $100 at one time.

CHAPTER FIFTEEN

How to Save Money on Credit Cards

Contrary to popular belief, you can use your credit cards towards your advantage to save money. Having credit cards does not mean you have to pay credit card companies to use credit cards. I will go over some simple tips to help you get the most out of your credit cards.

Free Short-Term Loan

Credit cards let you have short-term loans for free. This free period to have money is called grace period, during which your new purchases will not acquire interest charges if you pay your balance in full. In Canada, by law, credit card companies will have to provide a minimum 21 days grace period for all new purchases. I encourage you to take advantage of this free period by making all purchases on credit cards and paying the balance in full every month. Some credit companies offer more than 21 days grace period. Check with your credit card companies and ask them when the cut off date is or the last day to pay balances in full so it does not incur interest charges. Once you know that date, pay your credit cards each month in such a way that they get the payment before that date. What's the result? You get an interest free loan every month for life as long as you are paying off balances in full before the cut off date.

Annual Fees

In general, you should not have any credit cards with annual fees and should pay off your balances in full every month. However, this may not be always the case if you carry a balance. If you do carry a balance, a lower interest credit card with annual fees will save you money than a higher interest credit card with no annual fees. You will have to do your research to find out which credit cards will best suit your needs. There are free online tools and calculators to help you pick the right type of credit cards based on your needs. Also, I have produced a list of useful tools and calculators on A Dawn Journal, under the Personal Finance and Investing section.

Balance Transfers

From time to time, you will get promotional balance transfer offers via post mail, email, or on your online account screen offering very low interest rates (usually 1 to 5 percent) on your balance transfers or cash transfer into your bank account for 6 months to 1 year. If you know how to use this offer, you will be able to save a lot of money. I am not going to full details here, but you can read a full article I wrote on this on A Dawn Journal under Credit Cards and Debt Management section.

Reward Credit Cards

A reward credit card offers you reward points, travel points, or cash for using that credit card. These days, I see no point in using other than a reward credit card for your daily necessities. For example, on my travel reward card, I piled up about $500 in two years that I can use to purchase my next plane ticket. However, you will have to be picky to find the reward card that best suits your needs and offers you the most value. A reward card with an annual fee is OK as long as your reward value exceeds the fee you are paying.

Call For A Better Rate

It costs credit card companies to get a new customer, and letting a good customer go is the last thing in their minds. If you are with your credit card company for some time, have a good credit score, and you have a handful of transactions every month on your credit card, you may have some leverage to cut a deal with your credit card company. To get a lower interest rate, call your credit card company and ask. Remember the similar approach we discussed in Chapter Five. There is no reason you will not get a better rate than what you are currently paying. It works.

Is It Possible To Get An Annual Credit Card Without Paying An Annual Fee?

Yes, it is possible. Just like I mentioned above, if you are a customer that your credit company does not want to lose, they will waive your annual fee. All you have to do is call them and ask. I did it for my own credit card in the past. I posted an article on A Dawn Journal under Credit Cards and Debt Management Section on A Dawn Journal. Since then, readers tried it and it worked, as you will see in the comment section. However, you will have to call them every year to wave the annual fee.

Free Credit Card Features We Never Use

Most credit cards come perks and benefits that consumers never use. Why? Because most of us don't know that these features exist. It is estimated that only 15 percent consumers are fully aware of what they are getting and make full use of it. I will go over some of the common benefits you probably already have on your credit cards.

Free Purchase Warranty: This feature protects your purchases from against theft, loss, damage, etc. for 90 days or more, depending on your card company.

Free Extended Warranty: This feature doubles the manufacturer's warranty for an additional year.

Free Price Protection: Price protection refunds the difference if you see the same item you bought at a lower price somewhere else.

Free Collision/Loss Damage Waiver: If you rent a car with your credit card and decline the insurance the rental car company is selling you, this feature insures you for free in case of a loss or accidental damage.

Free Travel Accident and Baggage Claim: This feature protects you from travel accident injuries and baggage losses or delays.

You may not be able to get all of these free benefits in one card. I keep a combination of cards giving these features and I use a particular card for a specific feature when I need it.

CHAPTER SIXTEEN

How to Save Money on Taxes

I contemplated a few times whether or not I should add a chapter on taxation. It is somewhat difficult to write a chapter on taxes that will be suitable for global readers because tax rules widely vary from country to country. For that reason, I will keep our discussion at its minimal and simplest terms. Let's go over some tips that should work regardless of where you are.

File Your Return on Time

If you owe the government money, you will get penalized if you don't file your tax return on time. On the contrary, if the government owes you money, you can take your time to file whenever you want. For example, I am always late filing my tax return, as I always get refunds. The filing deadline in Canada is by the end of April, but I always end up filing in September. In some countries, you still might get charges late fee for filing late, even if the government owes you money, so check what are the rules in your country first.

Use All Available Tax Credits

There are so many tax credits available, but most people end up not claiming all that's available simply because it's not nearly impossible to know all the credits that can be claimed. What you can do? Always consult a tax professional to do your taxes, unless your tax return is super simple, such as you are a single working person living with your dog and there are no other income, savings, investments, persons involved in your life, and so on. It's not worth trying to save a few bucks, but losing more money on tax credits.

Use Government-Offered Plans To Reduce The Taxes You Pay

Each country has its own version of registered or government tax-sheltered plans where you can deposit money to get tax breaks in various ways. In North America, these are called RRSP, IRA, TSFA, etc. Make full use of these types of plans available in your country and utilise the tax saving opportunities government is providing for you.

Marriage and Tax Savings

There are various tax savings that exist for married or couples living together. These savings can be very simple to very complex. Consult a tax professional to find out which rules can be applied to your situation to save you money.

Investments and Tax Savings

Different types of investments attract different tax treatments. Find out what kind of investments get preferential tax treatments in your country and it to its full potential. For example, in Canada, Canadian stocks get preferential tax treatments on gains and dividends over foreign stocks or fixed-income securities.

Business and Tax Savings

If you own your own business, 90 percent of countries on Earth will treat you generously by giving huge tax breaks. If entrepreneurship is in you, start your own business and save lots of money on taxes. Visit www.EntrepreneurJourney.com for various business ideas and information.

Hire A Tax Professional

Whether your tax situation is simple or complex, I recommend hiring a tax professional to handle your taxes. There are myriads of tax deductions and credits available and these are changing frequently, every year. For a regular individual, it is not possible to keep track of all these changes. One of the many differences between rich and poor people is that rich people know how to use the tax system towards their advantages, but poor people miss the chance to use it.

Yes, there are software programs to do your taxes, but these programs can't know you personally to access your unique situation and figure out the best legal loopholes to save you on taxes. A good tax professional is like a good friend who can help you through different stages of your life. Don't worry about the money you spend on fees; it's worth it.

CHAPTER SEVENTEEN

How to Save Money on Travel or Vacation

I like to travel, like most other people, but regrettably the costs are rising every year. However, if you use the Internet to do your research and know a few techniques, you can save a lot of money on your travel or vacation. Let's go over some travel tips you can use to save you money.

Travel During The Low Season

Airfare cost is the most expensive segment of your travel expenses and you can cut it significantly if you travel during your destination's low season or off-peak time. Use the Internet to find out what is the off-peak time for the places you are traveling to. Another advantage of traveling during the low season that I enjoy is that it's not too crowded and easier to move around and go sightseeing.

Mind Which Days You Fly

You will also be able to save money on airfare by picking specific days of the week to fly. Flying volume is higher on Monday, Thursday, and Friday. If you avoid these days and fly other days you will get better deals.

Book Early

Early booking always saves you money. If you book your ticket 3 months to 1 year ahead, your savings will be higher than booking just before the trip.

A Package Saves You Money

Whether you are booking an all-inclusive vacation to Cuba, or booking a flight and hotel to Las Vegas, booking trips together as a package will save you money, rather than booking them separately.

Use Reward Cards

99 percent of banks and credit card companies offer travel reward cards these days. Use one or several reward programs available in your country and earn reward points to travel for free or partially free.

Never Use A Hotel or Airline's Own Website

If you use airline or hotels' own websites, you will end up paying more than 3rd party websites, unless they are offering a sale. Try a few websites such as Expedia, Kayak, etc. first before you book your trip, as prices can vary from site to site. There are sites that offer lowest price protection, so keep an eye out and if you find a better price you will get a refund for the difference.

Beware Currency Exchange Rates

Know your destination country's currency rate before you leave. An airport or hotel's own currency shop usually will not give you the best possible rates. What I have found out from various trips is that those small currency shops located outside offer the best rates in general. I only convert about $100 of my destination country's currency beforehand to keep it with me and I convert the rest at a currency shop in my destination country. Also, if you are using your credit cards you will get good currency rates, as credit card companies get preferential currency rates due to their high-volume transactions every day. But make sure you are aware of what your credit card companies are charging you in currency conversion fees when you use your credit cards in foreign countries.

Research Always Pays Off

International travel is far different than domestic travel. You are going to a place where everything is different and nothing is familiar to you. Make sure you do a lot of research on the Internet about your destination before you step out into unknown territories. Use common sense and research all the situations you may be dealing with. Here are some suggestions:

- How much would it cost to travel from the airport to the hotel?
- Should I be taking a taxi or avoiding a taxi, as in some countries taxis are not safe?
- Are there any tricks the local stores will do to make me pay more?
- Should I avoid any specific locations?
- Is it safe to stay outside the hotel in the evening?

CHAPTER EIGHTEEN

Smart Phone – Your Ticket to Savings

A smart phone can save you money in various ways. I will start this chapter with how you can talk/text on a smart phone for free, and then will discuss some more ways to save money using your smart phone. I can't possibly discuss everything a smart phone can offer to save you money. You should have an idea after reading this chapter and you can come up with more ways to save. There are no limits to saving, as there will be newer, innovative apps to save more in the future. I only named a few apps here, but there are many apps available to do the same job. Search on your smart phone's market (where you find or install apps) and try a few of them first before picking the one you want to stick to.

Make/Receive Calls/Texts For Totally Free

If you would like to spend zero dollars and still use your phone for talk and text, it is possible. The only drawback is you need to be connected to WiFi and will not be able to use your phone if there is no WiFi available. What I have noticed these days is that most stores, whether coffee shops or general stores, have WiFi. You need to install VOIP or Internet call apps on your phone. Some of these apps are Groove, Google Voice, Fongo, etc. These apps will give you a phone number, just like a real home phone or cell phone number, and you can use that number to receive and send texts or calls unlimited for free. So basically, you will have a functional phone that will work when you are at home or at any WiFi location.

Make/Receive Calls/Texts Paying Very Little

If you would like little more flexibility to have a cell phone network but don't want to pay a lot, you can consider using a pre-paid service along with a free Internet phone app. This way, you can make or receive emergency calls when you have no WiFi up to your pre-paid limit and can use an Internet app at home or WiFI locations other times. Some pre-paid services even offer unlimited inbound call and text. Based on your country, you are looking at about $15-$20 per month to spend for a pre-paid service.

Make/Receive Calls/Texts Paying A Little More

If you would like full flexibility to Make/Receive Calls/Texts at all times without paying a cell phone service, there is another option. You can subscribe to unlimited data from your phone carrier, instead of cell phone service, and use Internet phone at all times to Make/Receive Calls/Texts. You don't need to have access to WiFi with this option. Also, you don't even need a smart phone as a tablet that has SIM capability to subscribe to mobile data, such as Google Nexus tablets, can be used as a phone with this option. Based on your country, you are looking at spending $30 to $40 per month for unlimited data, which can still be lower than paying for a cell phone service in some places.

Scan Barcode To Save Money

Free barcode scanning apps like Red Laser, ShopSavvy, and Barcode Scanner can scan an item you are buying and let you know if the same item is available for lesser costs at nearest retailers based on your location.

Use Apps To Find Items On Sale or For Coupons

There are apps that can alert you for items on sale when you are near that store. Also, there are apps for coupons to save you money. I will name a few here such as RetailMeNot, Push A Deal, Shop to It, Groupon, ShopWise Canada, Checkout51, InstaCoupons, etc.

Walk Into Stores With Its Flyers In Your Pocket

Apps like Reebee, Flipp hold flyers from most big retailers. You can walk into any grocery or other stores knowing what's on sale and can choose to only buy those items are on sale.

Keep All Loyalty Cards Handy

Apps like CardStar, FidMe let you keep your loyalty card information on your phone and you can use them without carrying actual cards. In the long run, collecting loyalty points each time you buy something will save you money, as these points add up quickly if you use them.

CHAPTER NINETEEN

A Dawn Journal

A Dawn Journal is a globally-popular financial website that I started just before publishing my first book Invest Now. This site has a vast wealth of financial and some non-financial articles, including articles on saving money. I encourage you to visit A Dawn Journal at all times.

If you are reading this book, there are some sections on A Dawn Journal you might want to check out, as there are articles focused on how to save money on various things. I will post a few articles in this chapter from A Dawn Journal, as these are relevant with Money Hacks' theme.

Sample Postings

How to Save Money on Textbooks

Recently, I have noticed a lot of students are visiting ADJ. I can't mention names from the U.S. (because there are simply too many to name), but these Canadian institutions have highest concentration visiting ADJ: University of Manitoba, University of Toronto, York University, and Seneca College. I guess ADJ's simple language and easy-style articles are able to appeal to students. I thank you all for visiting this site and today's article has been specially written for you, whether you are a 20-year-old or 50-year-old student.

Buying textbooks is something every student goes through in their school career. An average textbook costs about $100 and each year you will be spending nearly $1000 on books. The objective of today's article is to show you how you can cut your textbook costs considerably by taking some simple steps. I will discuss this in two parts. In part one, I will show you what you can do to save money on textbooks. In part two, I will mention some websites that can save you money.

Save Money On Textbooks – Part 1

Borrow From Someone Else

Find someone who already completed the course and borrow their book. One thing you need to be aware of: Make sure your borrowed book still applies to the course. Publishers often change editions so old books no longer do the job. That's how they make money.

Buy Used

Buying used books is a great idea to save money but you need to find someone who is selling what you are looking to buy. You can check your school notice boards, newspaper ads, and online ads to find used books. I will be giving you some sites to find used books online in part two.

Photo Copy Those Pages You Need

Get a book from someone and copy those pages you need. Before doing this, make sure it does not violate any legal terms and conditions.

Trade books

Trade books with someone who has the books you need. This is simply giving someone the books he or she needs and taking from him or her the books you need.

Sell Books

Don't forget to sell your books once you are done with them. Your friends will likely want to buy them from you if you give them a good price.

Avoid Campus Bookstore

Avoid campus bookstore unless they have books on sale. Usually items are always overpriced at campus bookstores.

Group Buy

Take courses with your friends; divide the book's cost by how many of you are taking the course and each contributes to buy the required textbook. Make agreements beforehand stating how long each of you should keep the book during the term. During the exam, do group studies so all of you can use the book. Once you complete your term, sell the book and divide the money equally.

Use the Library

It may not be always possible to obtain a copy from the library; however, make sure to check the library before buying. The library has limits on how long you can keep a book. Taking a course with friends helps to keep books within your circle – another advantage of registering for courses with friends. Also, if your library has the book on reserve, you can go there and read it.

Campus website

You can buy and sell used books on your campus website. Since you will be dealing with other students, you will find good bargains and hard-to-find books because both buyers and sellers are dealing with the same institutions.

Original version posted on Monday, Nov 26, 2008, by A Dawn on the Internet. Visit A Dawn Journal for part 2 of this post..

Ten Wallet Tips You Need To Know Before Leaving Home

"Why carry something if you don't need it?" Twenty years ago, a senior taxi driver in New York City gave me that advice – the best wallet tip ever and I have been religiously following it ever since. Today, I will share some wallet or purse tips you should follow to make your life easier, simpler, and safer.

1. Go through your wallet and get rid of everything you will not use on a regular basis. There is no point carrying all the cards and receipts in your wallet. I keep only those that I use everyday. If I use a credit or debit card occasionally, I leave it home and only keep it with me when I will be using it.

2. At any point, you should know exactly what items are in your wallet. This way, if you lose anything you will be able to detect it right away, reducing your chances for being a victim if someone else gets ahold of your cards.

3. Make a list of everything you carry in your wallet. Write down your credit card number, customer service phone number, and anything else you would require to block your credit or debit cards in case of theft or loss of your wallet. Better yet, you can scan the back and front of all your cards as well. Keep this list handy at home, in a hotel safe, or online securely in such a way that you will have access to it when you need to call your financial institutions in case of emergency.

4. Do not carry your wallet in your rear pocket. Thieves use very sharp tools to cut pockets and it's a lot easier to cut when it's in your back or rear pocket.

5. Be careful and pay attention to what's going on around you. Thieves work together in crowded places and try to distract you by pushing you, causing artificial arguments among themselves, or anything else to cause distractions so they can use that split second to grab your wallet while you are distracted.

6. Keep some cash separated from your wallet in a different place on you. If you lose your wallet, this ensures that at least you will have some money to get home.

7. Do not keep your home or car keys in your wallet. If thieves get ahold of keys, they will be easily able to access your home or car because it's not hard to find information (home address on driver's license, vehicle information on insurance or registration card, etc.) leading thieves to further carry on their operations.

8. Do not write your PIN number on the back of your cards or carry it with you in your wallet. Also, do not use your date of birth, postal code, or your phone number as your PIN. If

thieves have your wallet, they will have access to enough information to guess your PIN by going through your wallet.

9. Do not leave your wallet in a jacket, coat, or anywhere else if you're checking out these items in a restaurant, movie theatre, or anywhere else.

10. If you are wondering what's in my wallet, here are the items I always carry with me if I am in Toronto:

- One bank card (Interac card)
- One credit card
- Driver's license
- Toronto Transit Commission Metropass

If I travel, I modify these items depending on where I am traveling.

NB – You do not need to carry your rewards or points card anymore as smart phone apps have the capability to carry these cards digitally on your smart phone.

Original version posted on Monday, Dec 8, 2011, by A Dawn on the Internet

How To Cut Down on Your Gas

Everyone knows that gas emissions are carbon dioxide emissions and the more emissions we have in the atmosphere, the worse global warming will be. While buying a hybrid is a great option, it is not an option for everyone. Some people have to juggle their own finances and are looking for ways to cut down on the gas that their conventional vehicle uses. Not only does cutting down on gas help the environment, it also helps all of us save money. Try these tips to make your wallet breath a sigh of relief, and to help the environment as well.

1. Most vehicles these days can handle ethanol-gas mixtures, usually at a rate of about 20/80, where the gas is made up of 20 percent ethanol and 80 percent gas. Using an ethanol mixture cuts back on your CO2 emissions, but it does not help your wallet.

2. Instead of doing errands several days of the week, try and consolidate your errands into just one day if possible. By doing this, you save yourself trips into town, which keeps you from spending too much money. Many drivers will make short trips into town each day to run their errands when a weekly trip will do just as fine.

3. When you are in town running errands, park in a central area and walk to all your errands. That way you are not starting and stopping your vehicle over and over, nor are you driving it everywhere. You also get some great exercise when you walk where you need to go, rather than drive there.

4. Idling your vehicle is bad news for the environment and it is just wasted money. When it is cold, you can let your vehicle run for a minute or so when you start it up, but that is all it needs. As well, you do not need to leave your vehicle running while you are in the store. Instead of going through the drive-thru, you can easily just go inside and get your food. It is usually less busy in there anyways.

5. Instead of driving, just walk to the store. If it is a beautiful day out, why not walk to the store and get some great exercise and fresh air? You can get most places pretty quick depending on where you live and you do not have to waste any gas.

6. Public transit is a great alternative because it allows you to catch a ride on a bus or subway for a fraction of what you would pay

for fuel. In addition, you no longer have to worry about a commute or driving; you can just sit back and read.

7. Carpooling is another popular option that many people choose. When you carpool, you share a vehicle with others and you drive only ¼th of the time to work. This is a good option that saves you money and lets you get to know your co-workers.

It is easy to save money, gas, and the environment when you use these tips to going green with your vehicle's gas.

Original version posted on Monday, July 28, 2014, by A Dawn on the Internet

6 Things You Can Do Right Now To Manage Your Credit Card Debt

Credit cards are a modern-day necessity, and it's unrealistic trying to survive without them. However, if you are unable to manage them, credit cards can take over your life. Let's look at 6 simple things you can do right now to take charge of your credit card debt.

Stop Charging – If you have credit card debt that you can't pay in full every month, do not charge anything on the credit card unless you have the money to pay it. This is your first step towards managing your credit card debt.

Avoid Making Late Payments - Always pay on time and never make a late payment. Late payments can affect your credit score. Pay at least the minimum if you are unable to pay the full for any given month. I have seen people not paying a 70-cents bill thinking it would not make sense to pay this small amount. They ended up paying a penalty for late payment and affecting their credit score. A small amount can drag you down a lot if it's not taken care of in a timely manner.

Call and Ask – Call and ask your credit card companies for a lower interest rate and waive any penalty fees you may have occurred. Optimize balance transfer offers to lower your interest on credit card.

Pay Extra Amount – Pay whatever extra amount, whether it's a small or a big amount, you can possibly arrange to pay towards your credit card balances every month. If you look at paying additional amounts in terms of longer time frame, it will accelerate your debt-free endeavour a lot faster.

Be Aware of Credit Repair – The Consumer Reporting Act has rules regarding how long accurate information can appear in a report and no credit/fix companies have the authority to remove, erase, or change this in a consumers' file. Beware of these companies claiming to fix your file.

Take Charge of Your Finances - Learn about managing money, investing, and building wealth for your financial future. There are many independent personal finance websites like A Dawn Journal, Canadian government websites, and U. S. government websites to help you build your financial roadmap.

Original version posted on Monday, Jan 5, 2012, by A Dawn on the Internet

How To Save Money in Retirement

As you get older, you are going to want to think of ways that you can save money in retirement. Saving money is very important because you will not have as much of an income coming in and you need to prepare for a lot of costs, including medical. While you may have a lot of money in the bank, that does not mean you should spend it without thinking.

So, how can you save money in your retirement so your savings go a long way?

1. First, you need to determine how much money you need each year. This should include your insurance costs, travel costs, and the cost of day-to-day activities.

2. Calculate how much money you have coming in from investments, your pension, your tax-deferred income like IRAs and more. You will need an income that equals about 75 per cent of your current pay, which means that if you made $100,000 a year, then you will need $50,000 to $75,000 a year.

3. Keep in mind the rise of inflation, which can vary between one to five per cent per year. The money you have now will not go as long of a way as it will in 20 years.

4. Talk with a financial planner about how much money you are going to need and ways that you can make your retirement savings grow over time. The financial planner will cost you money, but it will also earn you money and save you money.

5. Cut back on anything you do not need to spend money on. Go through your expenses and determine what you can cut back on. This is very important to do because you want to save money anywhere you can. If you do not need a second car in retirement, then sell the car and put the money into your retirement funds. Do you need the house you have or can you move to a smaller one?

6. You should also determine ways that you can bring extra money in. This does not include your investments or pension, but doing hobbies that will earn you money. If you enjoy working with clay, wood or stone, then you can make things that you can sell at a market. It is something you can do to fill

your spare time, which you have a lot of, and you are not working a full time job.

When you want to save money in retirement, you need to determine what you can cut back on, where you can make money and how you are going to live. Retirement is not like the rest of your life when you are dealing with money coming in at a regular basis. You do have money coming in, but it will not be as much money as you are used to, and that means you have to make adjustments in your life to meet that new requirement within your life. Retirement can be fun; you just need to know how to manage it properly.

Original version posted on Monday, Oct 28, 2010, by A Dawn on the Internet

CONCLUSION

A Wonderful Journey

It is hard to believe, but we are in the closing chapter of this book. I enjoyed every moment of writing it, and I hope you enjoyed every moment reading it. Since I published Invest Now, I have been contemplating publishing another paper book and have been working on it at a slow pace for the last few years. However, this year, in 2014, I decided to publish all my future books as eBooks from now on. As a result, Money Hacks is available only as an eBook on Amazon.

Where Do We Go from Here?

Paying less for most of things in life we need is not a miracle. It is a combination of knowledge and discipline. Reading this book and forgetting about it after a couple of days will not do you any good unless you start taking action. I will consider my work successful if this book can make you determined enough to save and improve your life by taking positive action toward your financial goals.

Aim For $100 Per Month In The Beginning

Based on the techniques I mentioned in this book, it is possible to save a lot of money. However, it is unrealistic to assume that everyone will be able to use each of the techniques in their countries. If you follow only some techniques to save on most costly items and services we need to survive, such as Internet subscription, cable TV service, cell phone service, transportation, clothing, and groceries, there is no reason you cannot save at least $100 a month, regardless where you live. In your notebook, write down your saving objectives or goals, including the procedures you would like to follow to achieve them. Write down every detail. Once every six months or once a year, go through your journal to see how you are doing and whether you need to change anything to reach your saving goals.

Emotion and Risk

Spending and saving can be emotional matters, and emotionally driven decisions can be risky. Don't be an emotional shopper. Avoid unnecessary spending by not making emotional decisions. Emotional decisions can be a recipe for disaster.

Feedback

Feedback is always welcome. Your opinions matter, and I would like to hear them. Communication fosters a connection between readers and author. Let me know if this book worked out for you—or even if it didn't. Let me know which parts of this book you find most helpful and which parts you think did not help and/or need more elaboration or clarification. Based on your feedback, I will update the future edition.

How to Contact Me

The easiest way to contact me would be to send me an e-mail. My e-mail address is adawn.net@gmail.com. Also, you can contact me by leaving a comment on my A Dawn Journal; I will reply right below your comments.

The Journey Is the Destination

Readers like you inspired me to write this book. I thought I would share valuable knowledge and hopefully change someone else's life. I believe in what I said, and every word in this book came out spontaneously. I enjoy writing for you, and my journey has taken me to my next trip: my third book. I have not decided yet what the name will be, but *Personal Finance Hacks* seems to be a good option at this moment.

You will encounter many personal finance related issues in your life. In my next book, I will be writing about some of the tips you can follow to improve and manage your finances every day, month after month. I will start working on my second book shortly after this book is published.

I hope to see you again, and until then, remember: Live for the journey, not for the destination. The journey *is* the destination.

MONEY HACKS:

How Small Changes Can Save Big Money

By Award-Winning Author Ahmed Dawn

The must-have guide for global savers. Money Hacks delivers surprisingly simple steps to save money.

Walk into stores with confidence knowing you can outsmart retailers to save money. Award-winning financial author Ahmed Dawn reveals practical steps you can take to save money through various walks in life. Jam-packed with timely information and timeless advice for the global readers, Money Hacks provides a realistic, doable plan to put you on the road to financial security by saving money.

Every time you spend money, you lose an opportunity to save money. To help you get started with saving money, this book will show you…

- Where to look in grocery store aisles to save money
- How to save at least $100 a month anywhere on earth.
- How to cut your Internet cable and still have Internet at home
- How to cut your cable wire and still watch HD channels on TV
- How it is possible to receive/make calls/texts on smartphones without paying anything
- And much more!

Money Hacks offers no-nonsense, precise, and to-the-point tools and motivation you need to start saving money for you and your family.

www.ingramcontent.com/pod-product-compliance
Lightning Source LLC
Chambersburg PA
CBHW070442220526
45466CB00004B/1752